A BEACON ✹ BIOGRAPHY

Stephen
Curry

Nicole K. Orr

PURPLE TOAD
PUBLISHING

Printing   1   2   3   4   5   6   7   8   9

A Beacon Biography

Angelina Jolie
Anthony Davis
Big Time Rush
Bill Nye
Cam Newton
Carly Rae Jepsen
Carson Wentz
Chadwick Boseman
Daisy Ridley
Drake
Ed Sheeran
Ellen DeGeneres
Elon Musk
Ezekiel Elliott
Gal Gadot
Harry Styles of One Direction
Jennifer Lawrence

John Boyega
Kevin Durant
Lorde
Malala
Maria von Trapp
Markus "Notch" Persson, Creator of Minecraft
Millie Bobby Brown
Misty Copeland
Mo'ne Davis
Muhammad Ali
Neil deGrasse Tyson
Peyton Manning
Robert Griffin III (RG3)
Stephen Colbert
Stephen Curry
Tom Holland
Zendaya

Publisher's Cataloging-in-Publication Data
Orr, Nicole K.
    Stephen Curry / written by Nicole K Orr.
        p. cm.
Includes bibliographic references, glossary, and index.
ISBN 9781624693960
1. Curry, Stephen, 1988—Juvenile literature. 2. Basketball players—United States—Biography—Juvenile literature. I. Series: Beacon biography.
 GV884.C88 2017
 796.323092

Library of Congress Control Number: 2017956809

eBook ISBN: 9781624693977

ABOUT THE AUTHOR: Nicole K. Orr has been writing for as long as she's known how to hold a pen. She is the author of several other titles by Purple Toad Publishing and has won National Novel Writing Month eleven times. Orr lives in Portland, Oregon, and camps under the stars whenever she can. When she isn't writing, she's traveling the world or taking road trips. Orr would probably lose a basketball game against Curry, but she just might beat him at Chinese checkers!

PUBLISHER'S NOTE: This story has not been authorized or endorsed by Stephen Curry.

CONTENTS

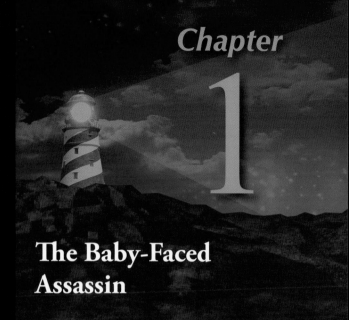

Superstar Steph Curry has helped his team, California's Golden State Warriors, break basketball records.

The Baby-Faced Assassin

Steph Curry lit up the June night. The Golden State Warriors' superstar guard delivered 34 points and then made an incredible clutch-shot. Curry's moves clinched a 2017 NBA championship series against Cleveland. It was the team's second NBA title in the last three years.

Klay Thompson buried a three-pointer in the championship clincher. Three of them, in fact. Golden State's other superstar guard wasn't break-the-scoreboard hot against Cleveland, but his long-range play made a difference. Curry and Thompson—the Splash Brothers—played to their reputations.

Curry and Thompson have been shooting their way to success for years. In 2015, the Splash Brothers (named for their three-point records) shot Golden State to a championship. In 2016, they helped produce the best regular-season record in NBA history (73-9), but lost to Cleveland in the championship series.

Payback came in 2017. Golden State lost six more regular-season games, but made up for it with a postseason run to remember. The team

Klay Thompson avoids a block. Like Curry, Thompson is the son of an NBA star.

blew through the playoffs with a 16-1 record, the best in NBA history. Their only loss came early in the best-of-seven series against Cleveland, but they won the final two games, including the 129-120 finale, to win the series 4 games to 1. They had become one of the best basketball teams ever.

Beyond that, Curry and Thompson combined for 678 three-pointers in the 2015–16 season, an NBA record for teammates. Entering the 2017–18 season, they had five straight years of at least 200 three-pointers, another NBA first.

Curry's talent on the basketball court may seem obvious now, but it wasn't always so.

He's too small. His eyes aren't good enough. He looks like a teenager. He'll be slower than everyone else in the sport. He weighs half of what the other players do. No one will take him seriously. He isn't and can't be his father. Pass him up. Let someone else have him.

Before he became a basketball star, many people made these harsh comments, and more, about Stephen Curry (STEH-fen KUR-ee). From the time he was a child, he had to fight past people's expectations of him. When coaches looked at him, they saw a little kid trying to impress.

When teams looked at him, they saw someone they couldn't depend on. When Curry looked at himself, he saw someone who couldn't be the star his father had been.

All of these obstacles could have discouraged Curry, but instead they gave him the courage to prove everyone wrong. When he was given the nickname "The Baby-Faced Assassin," he knew he'd done just that. He might have looked young and small, but he was a killer on the basketball court.[1]

As Curry got older, he grew taller—and he grew a beard. He exercised to gain strength and size. He got married and had two daughters. None of this changed what people thought. The nickname Baby-Faced Assassin wasn't going away. If he wanted to prove his value to those coaches, teams, and himself, he would have to do it in the one place he felt the most powerful.

He'd have to do it on the court.

Stephen Curry has always had a talent for leaping and can jump almost as high as some of the tallest NBA stars.

Dell Curry, Steph's father, played professional basketball for the Charlotte Hornets. The family moved from Akron, Ohio, to Charlotte, North Carolina, when Steph was two.

The Best Support in the World

"Well, you really gotta want it. You've gotta taste it. You gotta be able to smell it. I mean, you really gotta be hungry for it."[1]

This was advice that Dell Curry, Steph's father, gave him when he was just a kid. It was also more than that. This wisdom was shared during a Burger King commercial in which they both appeared. The advice was meant to make Steph want a hamburger, but it inspired him in other ways as well. The short video, made in the early 1990s, featured the two things that would become the most important to Steph Curry: family and basketball. They would shape the rest of his life.

Curry was born Wardell Stephen Curry II on March 14, 1988, in Akron, Ohio. He prefers to be called Stephen or Steph. Only his really good friends have permission to call him Wardell.

Steph was raised on basketball like most kids are raised on broccoli. His father, Dell, had played with the Utah Jazz, the Cleveland Cavaliers, the Charlotte Hornets, the Milwaukee Bucks, and the Toronto Raptors. Dell inspired countless young people to pick up a basketball, but none more so than his elder son, Steph.

The Curry family (left to right): Seth, Sonya, Sydel, Dell, and Steph. Steph is close to his family. As a kid, he'd watch emotional movies like A Walk to Remember *and* The Princess Diaries *with his sister. As an adult, he still remembers most of the lines.*

All five members of the Curry family loved sports. Basketball belonged to the men. When the boys were young, Dell would take Steph and Seth to his games, where they could watch and learn. The kids even got to play a little during the team's warmups. As adults, both Curry sons continued to play basketball. Seth went on to play for the Dallas Mavericks, while Steph played for the Golden State Warriors. As for the Curry women, it was volleyball. Sonya, Steph's mother, played volleyball for Virginia Tech. Sydel (sa-DELL) , his sister, played volleyball for Elon University in North Carolina.

Steph had a lot of support when he was a kid. When he became an adult, he built a new circle of support. This circle wasn't just made up of coaches and other players. In order for him to go on to the NBA (National Basketball Association), he'd need the best coach and the best teammates in the world.

He'd need a wife and kids.

Curry's yearbook photo from Charlotte Christian High School. Before one of his basketball games in high school, Curry was in the locker room getting ready. He got so excited about the game, he jumped in the air and hit his head on the ceiling! He had to get stitches.

Curry holds the trophy high at the 2017 Championship Parade. Later, while Steph high-fived his fans, his two little daughters waved and danced for them.

The Many Sides of Steph Curry

Steph met his wife, Ayesha Alexander, long before he fell in love with her. They were both going to the same Christian youth group at the Central Church of God. They almost never spoke to one another, and if not for the candy Maynards Fuzzy Peach, they might never have met.

Ayesha had moved to Charlotte, North Carolina, from Canada. Whenever she'd go to Canada for a visit, she'd bring back Canadian candy. One of these was Maynards Fuzzy Peach. While the candy introduced the boy and girl to each other, it was laughing over their first kiss that really brought them together.

"He was in mid-conversation and came flying at my face like a thief in the night," Ayesha said in an interview with *Parents*. "I mean, it was friend vibes . . . until I dodged his first kiss."[1]

In June 2011, the two were married. According to Curry, proposing to Ayesha was like a scene right out of a movie. "Yeah, it was like *The Notebook*," he explained, referring to the romantic story by Nicholas Sparks. Curry even described what the moment had looked like. "The plan was to act like we were going to a family cookout. So we pulled up to the house, and I stopped in the middle of the driveway, got down on my knee, and went into my spiel. Little did I know the whole family was looking out the window, videotaping the moment."[2]

The Curry couple had a fairytale beginning that only continued once they had children. "They started perfect. It's going perfect. They have perfect babies," explained Chris Strachan, a close family friend of the Currys. "They have perfect parents. They were perfect kids. It's a perfect relationship."[3] This opinion is shared by most fans of the growing Curry family, especially as they get to know Ayesha.

As an actor, Ayesha has her own set of fans. She's had small parts in the shows *Hannah Montana* and *Ballers*. She didn't find her passion until she started her own show called *Ayesha Homemade*, a cooking program on the Food Network. For one episode, she invited Steph and his brother Seth onto the show. Ayesha made Steph's favorite meal, sloppy joes. However, she wasn't making them in a bun as he was used to. To make the dish healthier, Ayesha stuffed the meat into green peppers. Steph's response to the idea?

"No, I can't do it."[4]

With Steph on one side wanting buns for his dinner and Ayesha on the other wanting peppers, the entire problem could be solved only one way: with basketball. They'd play the game Horse, but since the food would be getting cold, they'd play Buns instead to make the game go faster. This is just one example of how the couple handles disagreements.

As busy as Stephen and Ayesha are, they still both find time to be good parents. They have two daughters, Riley and Ryan. Keeping up with them can be more exhausting than playing a game on the court. "It's an event to get all four of us out of the house at once," Ayesha explained in the *Parents* interview. "When we get in the car and we've brought everything and everybody has socks on, it's like a dream come true."[5]

When Curry fans watch Steph's games on TV, they most likely see the player. He's strong and he's fast and he's one of the best basketball players in the world. What they don't see is the husband and father he is when he gets home. "The thing I love about him is that he's not too cool for school,"

Riley has always been a ham for the camera. Even when her father speaks to reporters at press conferences, she often steals the show with her bright smile.

Ayesha explained. "He'll get down on the floor and play with the girls. He'll put on dress-up clothes if he has to, and he's very patient, which is something I'm not."[6]

There are many sides to the Baby-Faced Assassin. There's the side that has made him an NBA star. There's the side coaches and other teams still underestimate when they first see him. There's the side that says he doesn't want his sloppy joe in a pepper. And there's the side that puts on dress-up clothes with his daughters. Does all of this take away from how well he does on the court?

Try watching one of his games and judge for yourself.

With Curry's jump shot taking as little as 0.4 seconds, Curry is setting new records. Most basketball players launch their basketballs in the same time it takes Curry to get the ball halfway to the basket.

Curry grew up knowing that he wanted to play basketball just like his dad and his brother. He also knew he wanted to play the big games, under the big lights, with the whole world watching. There wasn't one single moment that sparked his basketball dream. However, there was a moment when it almost ended.

Steph was already playing basketball when he was going to Charlotte Christian High School. His goal was to play in college, but as time went on, that seemed less and less likely.

In basketball, height and weight are important. Players need to be tall so they can reach the basket better, make shots from farther away, and see over other players. If they weigh too little, then the bigger players can easily knock them aside. When Steph was in eighth grade and dreaming of playing basketball in college, he was just 5 feet 6 inches tall and weighed only 125 pounds. He knew this was a problem. What he didn't know was that he also had a problem with his throw.

Basketball players often have to make long-distance throws to shoot for the basket or to pass the ball to another player. This requires a lot of power. Most of the time, these throws are made over the head. Curry, because of his size, had to begin all of his throwing motions from below his waist. With his arm starting the swing so low, he was giving other players a chance to swipe or block the ball. At first, he didn't realize just how big this issue was, but his father did.

"If you want to play in college," Dell told him, "you're going to have to bring the ball up and get it over your head."[1]

Steph took an entire summer off to fix the problem. He didn't study. He didn't meet with friends. He didn't even go to basketball games. He stayed at home, practicing with his father. Using the hoop they had in the backyard, the two men spent almost every day out there. Mornings, afternoons, and even hours into the night, they worked on Steph's jump shot. It was exhausting. It was upsetting. In the end, though, it was rewarding.

Together, father and son found a solution. When most players jump and launch the ball, they release it at the very top of their jump. Steph learned how to release the ball halfway through the jump. This gave the move extra power, but kept the other team from blocking or stealing the ball from him.

The hard work paid off. Steph played better on the court, and his body changed. By the time he graduated from high school, he was 6 feet tall and weighed 160 pounds.

Whether in their backyard or in a quiet stadium, Steph (left), Dell, and Seth Curry still find time to shoot some hoops together.

His chances of finding a team or school that wanted him were improving, but not by enough. Schools continued to pass him up because he was still too small. Dell Curry tried to help by contacting Virginia Tech. Dell had been one of Virginia Tech's best basketball players. He knew that this school sometimes signed small-time players or people who just needed a chance. They said no too.

While Virginia Tech was making its decision, a coach named Bob McKillop approached Steph. McKillop saw Steph's potential. He would later say to Steph's parents, "Your son will earn a lot of money playing this game one day."[2] He wanted Steph to play at Davidson College, just north of Charlotte. Steph had hoped for a bigger, better school, but he said yes.

Curry would finally get his chance to shine when Coach McKillop signed him to play for Davidson College.

It turned out that Davidson College was the best thing to happen to Steph, and Steph was the best thing to happen to Davidson College. The college hadn't won a game in the NCAA Division I Men's Basketball Tournament since 1969, but that changed in March 2008. Davidson not only made it into the tournament, they reached the Elite Eight—the highest bracket in their region. They lost the regional title to Kansas, who went on to win the championship.

After his stellar play in the tournament, Steph went back to Charlotte and was swarmed by fans. Everywhere he went, people knew who he was. In

Steph, flanked by his father and mother, proudly holds up his new jersey after signing with the Warriors. He chose the number 30 to honor his father, who wore the same number when he played for the NBA.

2009, he entered the NBA Draft and was chosen seventh overall by California's Golden State Warriors.

Curry took another summer off and practiced. He dribbled two balls at the same time that were different weights. He tossed a tennis ball in the air, dribbled a basketball behind his back, and then caught the tennis ball before it hit the floor. He dribbled with one hand while waving a heavy rope with the other. He wore goggles while practicing to force himself to use different parts of his vision.

When he next hit the court in 2012, he shocked the fans, the coaches, and the other players. Between the training he'd done and his latest growth spurt, pushing him up to 6 feet 3 inches, Curry felt he'd earned the right to be in 2013's NBA All-Star Game. When he was not chosen, he was upset.

Needing advice, he checked his cell phone. If Steph had a rough game, Coach McKillop would often send a text message. This time the text from McKillop read, "Sleep in the streets." This idea came from a famous player and coach named Kevin Loughery. "When life's rough and you're missing your shots or dealing with other kinds of disappointments, the only way to respond is to practice your heart out, even if it takes all night, leaving you locked out of your home and forced to sleep in the streets."[3]

Curry knew that "sleeping in the streets" meant staying out as long as he had to and working as hard as he had to. He'd slept in the streets many times before. He'd done it when he worked that summer in the backyard with his father. He'd done it again before his first season with the Warriors.

After another stretch of grueling training, Curry was rewarded again. He was chosen for the All-Star Game in 2014. Other wins started coming faster after that—including the championships in 2015 and 2017—but the most important change had already happened.

Finally, Steph Curry was a basketball star.

Teammate Kevin Durant looks on while Curry accepts the 2017 ESPY Award on behalf of the Warriors, who were named Best Team.

Curry worked with President Barack Obama on a program to fight malaria, and he continues to contribute to the cause. He has also played golf with the former president. In 2017 after the team's championship win, Curry decided not to visit the White House as part of a protest against inequality.

They'll Never Call Him Too Small Again

As important as basketball is to him, Steph Curry does find time to step off the court. When he isn't with his family, he likes to play golf. He's even played with Barack Obama. CNN asked Curry whether it was a relaxing experience or if he felt the pressure of being with the president of the United States. He said, "I couldn't relax at all," which would be due to the "25 Secret Service agents on every hole."[1]

Religion remains very important to Curry. During his pregame routine, he pounds his chest and points at the sky. It reminds him of his faith and to be grateful. He also has several religion-themed tattoos. One of these is a symbol that means "Love Never Fails." Ayesha has a matching one on her arm. Another tattoo Steph has includes the letters *WOE*, which stands for "Working on Excellence."

Basketball players have to be very careful when choosing the right shoes for the court. In order to make the right choice, Curry partnered with the athletic wear company Under Armour. Why did he choose Under Armour over the more popular choice, Nike? "I love the underdog mentality," he said in an interview with *CNBC*.[2]

Each year, Under Armour and Curry create new shoes named after the basketball player. In 2016, Under Armour released the Curry 3. These shoes come with customized sayings on them. Some feature one of Curry's mantras: "I can do all things." It comes from the Bible verse, "I can do all things through Christ who strengthens me." He used to write this mantra on his basketball shoes when he was a kid. Now fans everywhere can walk, run, or dribble a ball and remember where Curry places his faith.[3]

Curry believes in giving back to the world that has given so much to him. One of the biggest ways he's done this is by fighting malaria. This deadly disease is carried by mosquitoes, and people in tropical countries are most at risk for getting it. Through Nothing But Nets, Curry helps provide nets that protect people from mosquitoes. In 2013, he also began a Three-for-Three Challenge. Each time he scores a three-pointer during the season, he donates three of these protective nets to the Nothing But Nets campaign.

With Warrior Klay Thompson, Curry started the Splash Brothers Basketball Clinic, which benefits the Warriors Community Foundation. Curry has visited children's hospitals to say hello to kids with illnesses. He has also been known to give tickets to his games to youth who could not otherwise afford to come.

Each year, Curry hosts a celebrity golf tournament called ThanksUSA. The money it raises goes to the Ada Jenkins Center, a community center that promotes education and helps struggling families.

During the 2013–2014 basketball season, Curry was given an award for his charity work. Called the Seasonlong Community Assist Award, it is given to the NBA players who are the most charitable and driven to help their communities. When he accepted the award, Curry said, "Giving back to the community and those in need is something that has always been close to my heart and I am so grateful to have the opportunity to touch people's lives and hopefully impact them in a positive way."[4]

A lot has changed since Curry was a child. Gone are the days when people said he was too small or that his eyes weren't good enough. What do people say about Curry now?

People no longer doubt Curry's strength and talent on the court.

His bad shots are better than the good shots of other players. He doesn't put on an act for his fans. The NBA has never seen another player like him. He moves like a ballet dancer. He's shaped like a regular human, but he isn't.

A *Daily Beast* article said that Curry could "shoot the lights out"[5], and SB Nation called him "a basketball god in the flesh."[6]

When Curry looks at himself now, he likely no longer sees his own doubts or other people's expectations. He sees what was there all along, but only years on the court could bring out.

1988 Wardell Stephen Curry II is born in Akron, Ohio, on March 14.

1990s He is in two Burger King commercials with his father, Dell Curry.

2008 Steph helps Davidson College reach the top bracket in the Midwest Regional NCAA Men's Basketball Tournament. They fall to Kansas, 59–57.

2009 In the NBA Draft, Curry is picked seventh overall by the Golden State Warriors.

2011 Curry and Ayesha marry.

2012 Daughter Riley Elizabeth Curry is born on July 19.

2013 Steph Curry is passed up for the 2013 NBA All-Star Game. He signs an advertising contract with Under Armour.

2014 Curry receives the Seasonlong Community Assist Award. He is chosen for the NBA All-Star Game.

2015 He is again named to the All-Star Team. The Golden State Warriors win the NBA Championship. Curry sets a record with 286 three-pointers for the season. Daughter Ryan Carson Curry is born on July 10.

2016 He is again named to the All-Star Team. He is named the NBA Most Valuable Player by a unanimous vote.

2017 He is chosen to play in the All-Star Game for the fourth year in a row. The Golden State Warriors win another NBA Championship. Curry is named the NBA Most Valuable Player for the second year in a row.

STATISTICS

Regular Season Stats

Season	Team	Games	Rebounds	Assists	Steals	Blocks	Points
2009-10	Warriors	80	4.5	5.9	1.9	0.2	17.5
2010-11	Warriors	74	3.9	5.8	1.5	0.3	18.6
2011-12	Warriors	26	3.4	5.3	1.5	0.3	14.7
2012-13	Warriors	78	4.0	6.9	1.6	0.2	22.9
2013-14	Warriors	78	4.3	8.5	1.6	0.2	24.0
2014-15	Warriors	80	4.3	7.7	2.0	0.2	23.8
2015-16	Warriors	79	5.4	6.7	2.1	0.2	30.1
2016-17	Warriors	79	4.5	6.6	1.8	0.2	25.3

Playoffs Stats

Playoffs	Team	Games	Rebounds	Assists	Steals	Blocks	Points
2013	Warriors	12	3.8	8.1	1.7	0.2	23.4
2014	Warriors	7	3.6	8.4	1.7	0.1	23.0
2015	Warriors	21	5.0	6.4	1.9	0.1	28.3
2016	Warriors	18	5.5	5.2	1.4	0.3	25.1
2017	Warriors	17	6.2	6.7	2.0	0.2	28.1

Chapter One: The Baby-Faced Assassin

1. Reagan, Dillon. "Stephen Curry's Favorite Nickname: 'Baby-Faced Assassin.' " *Clutch Points*, June 2016. https://clutchpoints.com/stephen-currys-favorite-nickname-baby-faced-assassin/

Chapter Two: The Best Support in the World

1. Craggs, Ryan. "Here's a Young Steph Curry and His Dad in a Very '90s Burger King Commercial." *Thrillist*, January, 2016. https://www.thrillist.com/news/nation/steph-curry-and-dell-curry-in-90s-burger-king-commercial

Chapter Three: The Many Sides of Steph Curry

1. Shipnuck, Alan. "Stephen Curry and Wife Ayesha on Marriage, Kids and Their Matching Tattoos." *Parents*, n.d. http://www.parents.com/parenting/celebrity-parents/moms-dads/stephen-curry-wife-ayesha-on-marriage-kids-matching-tattoos/
2. Ibid.
3. Thompson, Marcus, II. "Stephen Curry in Middle School: The Origin of the Baby-Faced Assassin." *Bleacher Report*, April 2017. http://bleacherreport.com/articles/2695972-stephen-curry-in-middle-school-the-origin-of-the-baby-faced-assassin
4. Desantis, Rachel. "Ayesha's Homemade Premiere: Steph and Ayesha Battle Over Buns." Entertainment Weekly, October 19, 2016. http://ew.com/article/2016/10/19/ayesha-curry-homemade-food-network/
5. Shipnuck.
6. Ibid.

Chapter Four: Sleeping in the Streets

1. Thompson, Marcus, II. "Stephen Curry in Middle School: The Origin of the Baby-Faced Assassin." *Bleacher Report*, April 2017. http://bleacherreport.com/articles/2695972-stephen-curry-in-middle-school-the-origin-of-the-baby-faced-assassin
2. Ibid.
3. Zeidel, Andrew. " 'Rising Above' Excerpt: Stephen Curry." *Sports Illustrated Kids*, May 23, 2016. https://www.sikids.com/si-kids/2016/05/23/rising-above-excerpt-stephen-curry

Chapter Five: They'll Never Call Him Too Small Again

1. Zaru, Deena. "Steph Curry Dishes on Trash-Talking with Obama." CNN, August 20, 2017. http://www.cnn.com/2015/08/20/politics/steph-curry-obama-golf-trash-talking-ray-allen/index.html
2. Eisen, Sara. "Stephen Curry Speaks Out on New Under Armour Deal." CNBC, September 16, 2015. https://www.cnbc.com/2015/09/16/stephen-curry-of-the-golden-state-warriors-speaks-out-on-new-under-armour-deal.html?view=story&%24DEVICE%24=native-android-mobile
3. Straeter, Kelsey. "Stephen Curry Sports 'I Can Do All Things' Bible Verse on Under Armour Shoes." *Faith It*, February 24, 2016. http://faithit.com/america-is-freaking-out-over-the-message-spotted-on-steph-currys-new-under-armour-shoes-spiritual/
4. "Stephen Curry Receives NBA's 2013–14 Kia Community Assist Seasonlong Award." *NBA.com*, May 28, 2014. http://www.nba.com/warriors/news/curry-community-assist-award-20140528/
5. Silverman, Robert. "Why Steph Curry Scares NBA Legends." *Daily Beast*, March 2, 2016. http://www.thedailybeast.com/why-steph-curry-scares-nba-legends
6. Ziller, Tom. "Behold Stephen Curry and the Warriors in Their Purest Form." *SB Nation*, February 2016. https://www.sbnation.com/nba/2016/2/28/11128724/stephen-curry-warriors-behold-pure-gods

Books

Christopher, Matt. *On the Court . . . with Stephen Curry.* New York: Hachette Book Group, 2017.

Shea, Therese. *Stephen Curry: Basketball's MVP.* Berkeley Heights, NJ: Enslow, 2017.

Striking Gold: Golden State Warriors NBA Champions. Stevens Point, WI: KCI Sports, 2015.

Zuckerman, Gregory, and Elijah Zuckerman. *Rising Above: How 11 Athletes Overcame Challenges in Their Youth to Become Stars.* New York: Penguin Group, 2016.

Works Consulted

"13 Surprising Facts About NBA Star Steph Curry." *Sports Drop,* January 2016. http://thesportsdrop.com/13-surprising-facts-about-nba-star-steph-curry/

Chase, Chris. "13 Sharpshooting Facts About Steph Curry." *Fox Sports,* June 2017. http://www.foxsports.com/nba/gallery/steph-curry-facts-shoes-golf-salary-warriors-nba-finals-record-lebon-three-point-060117

Flessa, Maria-Elpida. "Stephen Curry Trivia: 39 Interesting Facts About the NBA Superstar!" *Useless Daily,* September 2016. https://www.uselessdaily.com/sports/stephen-curry-trivia-39-interesting-facts-about-the-nba-superstar/#.WbjJ0BmGPrc

Morris, Benjamin. "Stephen Curry Is the Revolution." *Five Thirty Eight,* December 2015. http://fivethirtyeight.com/features/stephen-curry-is-the-revolution/

Persaud, Melissa, and Maurice Peebles. "30 Things You (Probably) Didn't Know About Steph Curry." *Complex*, November 2015. http://www.complex.com/sports/2015/11/things-you-didnt-know-steph-curry/

Tsuji, Alysha. "Steph Curry Throws Basketball at Dad, Dell Curry, Who Then Drills Deep 3-Pointer." *For the Win*, February 2017. http://ftw.usatoday.com/2017/02/steph-curry-dell-curry-3-pointer-deep-shot-family-warriors-nba

Warond, Alonzo. "10 Amazing Facts You Didn't Know About Stephen Curry." *Fadeaway World*, December 11, 2016. http://fadeawayworld.com/2016/12/11/10-amazing-facts-you-didnt-know-about-stephen-curry/

On the Internet

The Ellen Show: "Steph Curry Interview"

https://www.youtube.com/watch?v=VLX-I39LVjo

The Golden State Warriors

http://www.nba.com/warriors/

The Splash Brothers

https://www.facebook.com/supersplashbros/

Steph Curry and Under Armour

https://www.underarmour.com/en-us/steph-curry-collection/g/325t

assassin (uh-SAS-in)—In sports, a player who blocks or scores suddenly and by surprise.

bracket (BRAK-it)—In a tournament, a chart that shows how teams are paired. The winners of each pair play until there is a champion.

draft (DRAFT)—A yearly event during which professional teams choose promising athletes to play for them.

Elite Eight (ee-LEET AYT)—The top two teams in NCAA Basketball's four regions.

Final Four (FY-nul FOR)—The top teams in each of NCAA Basketball's four regions.

jump shot—In basketball, a shot made by jumping into the air and releasing the ball at the peak of the jump.

malaria (muh-LAYR-ee-uh)—A deadly disease spread by mosquitoes.

mentality (men-TAL-ih-tee)—A way of thinking.

NBA—National Basketball Association—The organization that governs professional men's basketball.

NCAA (EN-SEE-DOUBLE-AY)—National Collegiate Athletic Association—The organization that governs college sports.

obstacle (OB-stih-kul)—Anything that stands in the way of reaching a goal.

potential (poh-TEN-shul)—A person's ability to be great.

pregame routine (PREE-gaym roo-TEEN)—A set of actions that a player normally does to get ready for a game.

reputation (reh-pyoo-TAY-shun)—The actions or traits a person is known for.

spiel (SPEEL)—A long speech.

three-pointer (THREE-POYN-ter)—In basketball, a shot taken from beyond the usual shooting area. From this far, the shot is worth three points instead of the normal two points.

unanimous (yoo-NAN-ih-mus)—Having the agreement of all voters.

underdog (UN-der-dog)—A team or person who is predicted to come in second or last.